The Inclusive Leader's Playbook

THE WORK OF THE INCLUSIVE LEADER ™

Susan MacKenty Brady

and

Elisa van Dam

Illustrated by

Loe Lee

ISBN: 978-1-7375159-0-6

Simmons University
Institute *for*
Inclusive Leadership

www.inclusiveleadership.com

CONTENTS

What are diversity, inclusion and equity?   2

What is the work of the inclusive leader?   4

The 6 actions   6

Understand bias   8
Understand bias: action plan   10
Value equity   12
Value equity: action plan   14
Partner for success   16
Partner for success: action plan   18
Advocate for belonging   20
Advocate for belonging: action plan   22
Sponsor   24
Sponsor: action plan   26
Make change   28
Make change: action plan   30

Wrapping it up   32

About the authors   34

Introduction

What do inclusive leaders actually do? What does it really mean to lead inclusively? If you sometimes wonder how to put inclusive leadership into practice, you aren't alone! This guide shares what we've learned from our research, conversations with experts, and our own personal successes and failures on our journeys to becoming more inclusive leaders. We've distilled it all down and created a playbook that we hope will help you increase engagement, foster creativity and innovation, and benefit from all of the talent in your organization.

Susan MacKenty Brady
Elisa van Dam

What are diversity, equity and inclusion?

There are lots of different metaphors to explain the differences between diversity, equity and inclusion. We like this metaphor of a party.

DIVERSITY

When we talk about diversity, we often mean that within the organization there are people who represent lots of different dimensions of diversity. In this metaphor, diversity means ensuring the invitation list includes representatives from many different social identities.

INCLUSION

Having lots of different people in a room doesn't mean that all of them feel included. In organizations, inclusion means making an effort to ensure everyone's voice is heard and everyone feels they belong. At the party, it's making sure everyone is engaged and enjoying themselves.

EQUITY

Equity is about systems that ensure everyone has equal access to opportunities and is treated according to their needs. For the party, it could mean creating a planning process that ensures the music and food represent many different cultures. It could even mean being deliberate about seating people from different backgrounds together.

What is the work of the inclusive leader?

Inclusive leaders care about diversity, equity, inclusion, belonging, and allyship, as well as many other aspects of leadership. Becoming an inclusive leader involves taking action on three levels:

LEVEL 1

Becoming aware

This is all about the work you do on yourself to increase your own understanding and awareness.

LEVEL 2

Becoming an ally and upstander

This is about actions you take to support others.

Becoming a change agent

This is about changing systems.

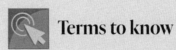

Terms to know

Unearned privilege is when you don't face certain obstacles, not because of merit or hard work, but because of a social identity that you share with the majority population.

A good metaphor is that unearned privilege is like a tailwind that pushes you forward in ways you may not even recognize or notice. People who don't benefit from that unearned privilege face strong headwinds that impede their progress.

The 6 actions

Each inclusive leadership level involves two actions:

LEVEL 1	LEVEL 2

BECOMING AWARE

BECOMING AN ALLY AND UPSTANDER

1 **UNDERSTAND BIAS** Increase awareness of biases, both conscious and unconscious	2 **VALUE EQUITY** Recognize the problems of historic systems of privilege and oppression; appreciate the benefits of dismantling them	3 **PARTNER FOR SUCCESS** Actively support and advocate for women and other underrepresented groups	4 **ADVOCATE FOR BELONGING** Create an environment where everyone feels uniquely seen, heard, and valued

LEARNING & SELF-REFLECTION

LEARNING & SELF-REFLECTION

BECOMING A CHANGE AGENT

HOW YOU GROW

Just as you have to learn to walk before you can run, you need to have a good understanding of your own biases in order to be an effective upstander and ally. That doesn't mean you stop doing Action 3 when you move into Action 4. Instead, you will be incorporating each new action while continuing to engage in the ones that came before.

Let's look at each of these actions in more detail.

Understand bias

Bias can invisibly shape our thinking, including our ideas about who should be a leader. Understanding how bias affects decisions allows us to make better choices.

YOUR WORK:

Look inward: Examine your own belief system to uncover the unconscious, implicit and explicit biases that are shaping your actions and decisions. Deepen your awareness of the ways biases may be shaping other people's actions and beliefs.

Look outward: In addition to the visible characteristics that we often think about such as race, ethnicity, gender, and age, there are many other characteristics that are important to who we are and how we show up. These include educational background, sexual orientation, family status, class, and many others.

 Diversity is about all the ways that human beings differ from one another. It's important to recognize that diversity includes so much more than the things we can see.

 Social identity is the term we use to describe different dimensions of diversity, because they describe a person's sense of identity based on what groups they belong to.

Understand bias: action plan

REFLECT:

- What messages did I receive when I was growing up about different races and ethnicities? What messages did I receive about gender? What about other social identities?

- What social identities are important to me at work? Which identities may give me advantages, and which may give me disadvantages?

- How can I become more aware of my own biases and how they may be impacting my decisions?

- Where am I in my understanding of different social identities? Which ones do I understand fairly well? Which would I like to learn more about?

- How can I learn more about different social identities?

TAKE ACTION:

- Take some Implicit Association Tests at implicit.harvard.edu

- Find opportunities to discuss and share thoughts about your social identities with your team

- Read widely on related topics; visit inclusiveleadership.com for suggestions.

- Seek out media of all kinds from creators from underrepresented groups

- Create practices and habits that help you recognize when bias tends to crop up for you so you can mitigate its impact

MY ACTION PLAN:

What do I want to do?

How will I know I'm making progress?

What are the obstacles that I might face in addressing this issue?

How will I overcome those obstacles?

Who can help me?

What are the first 2 – 3 concrete steps that I can take?

How will I stay accountable?

What did I learn from taking this action?

Value equity

Leaders create, sustain and improve systems to get work done. Inclusive leaders expand that work to examine how systems may cause inequity by having a different impact on different populations.

YOUR WORK:

Get informed: Actively deepen your understanding of the history and the current context around different dimensions of diversity, including gender, race, sexual orientation, ability, class, age, etc. Look at the ways that systems have historically privileged some people and oppressed others, and how those systems continue to create inequity today.

 Micro-inequities are the small ways that biases show up as differential treatment of people who aren't in the majority group. It might be leaving someone off of a meeting invitation, or rolling your eyes when someone is talking. Each individual situation might seem inconsequential, but over time they add up—it's like drops of water wearing away a stone.

 Emotional tax describes the consequences of being in an environment where you face the possibility of discrimination, bias and micro-inequities. People in this situation "put their shields up" and mentally prepare themselves to deal with these issues. Of course this preparedness is stressful and comes at a cost.

Value equity: action plan

REFLECT:

- What social identities give me unearned privilege at work?
  In my community? At home?

- Why are inclusion and equity important to me? What do I believe about
  equity? What are my values around equity?

- How can I be more aware of differential treatment of people who are
  traditionally underrepresented?

TAKE ACTION:

- Seek out mentors who have different social identities from yours

- Join an employee resource group or other network for a social identity
  you don't share; attend events to listen and learn

- Learn about the additional challenges facing women of color and
  women from other underrepresented groups

- Read widely on related topics; visit inclusiveleadership.com for
  suggestions

- Help people who share your privileged identity to recognize and
  understand their own privilege

MY ACTION PLAN:

What do I want to do?

How will I know I'm making progress?

What are the obstacles that I might face in addressing this issue?

How will I overcome those obstacles?

Who can help me?

What are the first 2 – 3 concrete steps that I can take?

How will I stay accountable?

What did I learn from taking this action?

Partner for success

Maximize your team's success by making sure all voices are heard, so you have the full benefit of everyone's wisdom and experience.

YOUR WORK:

Give voice to others: In situations where your social identity gives you unearned privilege, amplify the voices and increase the visibility of people who don't "look like" you. Educate other people who share your social identity and help them correct biased and discriminatory behavior.

 Ally is a term often used to describe a person who supports the advancement of someone from a different social identity—for example men as allies for women, white people as allies for Black, Indigenous, Latinx, Asian and other people from underrepresented racial and ethnic groups.

 Upstanders are people who speak or act in support of someone else, especially if that person is being ignored or attacked. When you partner with someone to support their success, you will likely act as both an ally and upstander.

Partner for success: action plan

REFLECT:

- Why is being an ally important to me?

- How am I already acting as an ally? For what groups?

- What opportunities do I have to engage in allyship?

- When did I have an opportunity to be an ally, but I didn't? What would I do differently next time?

- When am I making assumptions about what someone else may want or need or experience? How can I learn more about their interests and concerns?

TAKE ACTION:

- Amplify underrepresented voices in meetings and give credit for their contributions

- Encourage underrepresented colleagues to be more visible and celebrate their accomplishments

- Ask colleagues and direct reports about barriers at work and at home; allow them to share their experiences, be empathic, and address their concerns

- Ask which ally behaviors people from underrepresented groups find most effective and why

- Champion and support the development of other allies

- Make the business case that everyone benefits if the organization has better equity and inclusion

- Increase the visibility of other allies and their impact

MY ACTION PLAN:

What do I want to do?

How will I know I'm making progress?

What are the obstacles that I might face in addressing this issue?

How will I overcome those obstacles?

Who can help me?

What are the first 2 – 3 concrete steps that I can take?

How will I stay accountable?

What did I learn from taking this action?

Advocate for belonging

By creating a culture of belonging, you stimulate creativity, innovation, and engagement. Belonging means feeling accepted, secure and supported. It's the opposite of fitting in, which means being like everyone else. The difference between belonging and fitting in is like the difference between a salad, where each ingredient is distinct and makes up a harmonious whole, and a stew, where everything tastes the same.

YOUR WORK:

Foster psychological safety and authenticity: Create an environment where everyone feels appreciated and respected for who they are, and they don't have to hide aspects of their identity. Create a sense of trust and allow people to take risks and make mistakes without fearing they will be punished. Make sure that everyone's contributions are seen and valued.

Psychological safety is the belief that you won't be ridiculed or punished for speaking up, expressing an unpopular opinion or making a mistake.

Covering means hiding part of who you are because that aspect of your identity tends to disadvantage you. For example, someone who is gay might not be out at work for fear of being discriminated against.

Advocate for belonging: action plan

REFLECT:

- When have I felt like I didn't belong? What was the impact on how I felt, how I was able to accomplish my goals for the situation?
- How do I foster engagement of everyone on my team?
- How do I measure and value results rather than how many hours are spent at work / in the office?
- How am I contributing to psychological safety on my team / in my organization?
- How am I diminishing psychological safety on my team / in my organization?

TAKE ACTION:

- Create processes that ensure all team members have an equal voice and equal access to opportunities
- Implement ideas to increase psychological safety, such as sharing how you have benefited from feedback and what you are working to improve
- Call out biases and stereotypes in a way that is constructive and leads to a larger conversation
- Practice courage and vulnerability by talking about emotions, sharing when you are uncertain or afraid, and asking for what you need
- Encourage others to be vulnerable as well

MY ACTION PLAN:

What do I want to do?

How will I know I'm making progress?

What are the obstacles that I might face in addressing this issue?

How will I overcome those obstacles?

Who can help me?

What are the first 2 – 3 concrete steps that I can take?

How will I stay accountable?

What did I learn from taking this action?

Sponsor

Championing someone from an underrepresented group is one of the most powerful actions a leader can take to increase diversity, equity, inclusion and belonging.

YOUR WORK:

Advocate actively: Use your relationship capital to actively advocate for someone from an underrepresented group. Look for opportunities to provide your sponsees with stretch assignments, promotions, and visibility to senior leaders.

 A sponsor is someone who puts their reputation on the line to support someone else's advancement. The person they are sponsoring is sometimes called their "sponsee." Sponsors are generally one or more levels above their sponsees in the organizational structure, so they're in the room when opportunities are discussed.

 A mentor is someone who provides advice and support and can act as a sounding board. Mentors may also act as sponsors.

Sponsor: action plan

REFLECT:

- Who am I already sponsoring? How much do they "look like me"?
- Who am I already mentoring? How much do they "look like me"?
- How can I broaden my network of potential mentees and sponsees?
- Why is being a sponsor important to me? To my organization?
- How can I increase my understanding of the interests and ambitions of the people I mentor and sponsor?

TAKE ACTION:

- Identify opportunities to speak up on behalf of underrepresented talent
- Seek mentoring relationships across dimensions of difference
- Identify people who might be good candidates for sponsorship; get to know them professionally and personally including their body of work, their strengths, and their ambitions
- Introduce sponsees to people who can give them a broader perspective and increase their visibility
- Speak up and create opportunities for your sponsees

MY ACTION PLAN:

What do I want to do?

How will I know I'm making progress?

What are the obstacles that I might face in addressing this issue?

How will I overcome those obstacles?

Who can help me?

What are the first 2 – 3 concrete steps that I can take?

How will I stay accountable?

What did I learn from taking this action?

Make change

Identify opportunities and take the lead on making changes that mitigate the impact of bias and inequities on systems and processes.

YOUR WORK:

Take the initiative: Develop and drive changes that level the playing field. Look at processes and procedures and consider how they might unintentionally advantage some people and disadvantage others.

Although this is the highest level of our model, you don't have to be at the top of the organization to do this work; remember that a lot of changes start at the grassroots level.

 Small wins are changes that you can make within your own sphere of influence. One example is creating norms around how meetings are run to make sure all voices are heard. The great thing about small wins is that they often gain momentum and lead to larger changes.

Make change: action plan

REFLECT:

- What does our employee population look like in terms of diversity of social identities?
- What does our leadership look like – is it gender balanced? Are other historically underrepresented groups included?
- What processes do we have in place to guard against bias in decision making?
- What mechanisms are there to support and encourage women and other underrepresented groups on their leadership path?
- What are our talent management processes and how can we make them more unbiased?
- How do underrepresented talent have access to developmental opportunities, including feedback, training, stretch assignments? Are the standards the same for all groups?

TAKE ACTION:

- In all talent management decisions, take steps to create more diversity of background and thought
- Identify opportunities for small wins that can help decrease equity headwinds
- Champion, support, and defend equity initiatives and encourage others to join you
- Get the facts about your organization – what are the representation numbers, what efforts are underway to increase equity?

MY ACTION PLAN:

What do I want to do?

How will I know I'm making progress?

What are the obstacles that I might face in addressing this issue?

How will I overcome those obstacles?

Who can help me?

What are the first 2 – 3 concrete steps that I can take?

How will I stay accountable?

What did I learn from taking this action?

Wrapping it up

The work of an inclusive leader is never done. The foundation for all of these actions is learning and self-reflection. That means making an ongoing commitment to deliberate practice and evaluating your impact. It also means requesting, accepting, and processing feedback from others on how you're doing.

The action planning pages in this workbook can help guide you to taking meaningful actions. They aren't intended to suggest that you should be working on all 6 Actions at once! Pick one or two areas to focus on at any given time. We also suggest you look for things you can stop doing, to make room in your schedule for these new actions.

As you progress, you will begin to uncover nuances that we haven't covered here. You may also discover that you are farther along the path when it comes to some social identities than others. For instance, you may discover that you're ready to act as a sponsor across racial differences, while you're just starting to understand historic systems of privilege and oppression when it comes to people who have a disability.

Remember: no one does this perfectly, and that's OK. The important thing is to start somewhere, do the best you can, and keep learning and growing over time. It's all part of the process!

About the authors

SUSAN MACKENTY BRADY

Susan is CEO of the Simmons University Institute for Inclusive Leadership and the Simmons University Deloitte Ellen Gabriel Chair of Women and Leadership. Susan ignites, inspires and advises executives to foster a mindset of inclusion and create a culture of equity in their organizations. She is the author of *Mastering Your Inner Critic and 7 Other High Hurdles to Advancement: How the Best Women Leaders Practice Self-Awareness to Change What Really Matters* (McGraw-Hill, November 2018), and *The 30-Second Guide to Coaching Your Inner Critic* (Linkage, 2014). Susan has been featured on ABC's Good Morning America and has keynoted or consulted at over 500 organizations worldwide.

ELISA VAN DAM

Elisa is Vice President for Allyship & Inclusion at the Simmons University Institute for Inclusive Leadership. Drawing on her expertise in gender equity and women's leadership, she creates innovative programming that develops the mindset and skills of leaders at all stages of life so they can foster gender parity and cultures of inclusion. Elisa is a co-author on several publications, including *The Importance of Authenticity in the Workplace* (July 2021) and *Women's Experiences with "Male Allies"* (November 2018).

LOE LEE [ILLUSTRATOR]

Loe Lee is a Chinese-American illustrator in New York City who marries whimsical themes with everyday scenes. She's had the pleasure of working with corporations and local businesses alike, adding a splash of magic to their projects and spaces. Loe is represented by Gerald & Cullen Rapp.

Made in the USA
Las Vegas, NV
21 April 2022

47797786R00024